TRAINING YOU
TO TRAIN YOUR CAT

TRAINING YOU
TO TRAIN YOUR CAT

Leon F. Whitney, D.V.M.

Photographs by Stephen Hodio

DOUBLEDAY & COMPANY, INC.
GARDEN CITY, NEW YORK

FOREWORD

Ever since I was a boy, up until a few years ago, I used to wonder why nobody trained cats. I mean cats as we know them in our homes. I've seen a few stage acts and two on television. I heard one trainer say on a television show that the reason he had so many cats on his show was that a cat could be taught only one trick.

Perhaps, I thought, the reason why everyone believes cats can't be trained is that those people have no knowledge of newer practical psychological techniques. And that, I'm sure now, is the reason. They had been thinking in terms of forcing and rewards and punishment, when they should have known about fulfilling needs, signals, responses, and reinforcements.

This is not a long book; it could be, were we to delve into much of what is known about cat psychology. But I think that it contains what you need to know about training your cat. There are enough illustrations on a fairly wide variety of responses so that you can improvise in conditioning your cat to respond in other ways which may occur to you.

My thanks go out to all of those who have helped me so much:

to my son, Dr. George D. Whitney, who supplied the four cats I used; to Stephen Hodio for his patience and excellent photography; to my secretary, Florence Gamble; to my grandson, Jonathan B. Taylor, for his suggestions in regard to the manuscript; but most of all to my wife, who helped in so many ways.

Leon F. Whitney, D.V.M.

ORANGE, CONNECTICUT

CONTENTS

TRAINING YOU
TO TRAIN YOUR CAT

NOTE

In this book you will find the female cat called a *catta*. Until I used the word, it seems incredible that we had no word for her. The male was a tom. True, cat fanciers who show cats have called the female a queen, but they reserve it for show cats only. Your cat and mine have always been just female cats. The female of the dog is bitch; of cattle, cow; of the horse, mare; of the goat, nanny, etc. I first used catta in *The Complete Book of Cat Care*, and it has caught on so rapidly that one frequently sees it used by other writers who have appreciated having, at last, "a word for it." So now you too have a word for it.

Chapter One

Do Owners Train Cats
or Vice Versa?

"Of all God's creatures there is only one that cannot be made slave to the lash. That one is the cat. If man could be crossed with the cat it would improve man, but it would deteriorate the cat."—Mark Twain.

Mark Twain was expressing the belief of practically every human being who had known or owned a cat. He and all the others were right up to half a century ago, because all animal training was based on two important factors.

The first was that animals—dogs particularly—were bred by selection to inherit certain behavior patterns and such companions of man needed little training; they performed naturally. No one had to train a bird dog to hunt birds, keep its head high and stop to point when it scented a bird. No one had to train a scent hound to put his nose to the ground and follow the scent left by some animal and to bay as he followed. No one would have known how to train a dog to do it.

The second fact about animal training in years gone by was that it was all a matter of *forcing* the animal to do something.

Horses were *broken,* steers were forced to work in yokes. Dogs were trained, or kennel-broken. Everything was negative.

There was something about cats which defied breaking. People called it *independence.* "Cats are too independent to be trained." How many times have you heard that expression? *Trained* being, in the speaker's idea, another word for *broken.*

Well, there definitely is "something about cats" which seems to defy *breaking.* Hurray for cats! But don't let the old adage throw you, because there is nothing about cats that is so different from other species as to defy the application of a method about which Mark Twain and all the other millions who have believed cats could not be trained, knew nothing.

And you are now going to learn about this method and use it, I hope, to train your cat. You are going to disprove the opinion of hundreds of millions of people past and present, including Mark Twain. With what they knew they couldn't train their cats; with what you will soon know you'll find how wrong they all were and how much fun there is in this useful knowledge.

I must say that I feel sorry for cats and for cat-owners. For cat-owners because they are overlooking a source of great fun and satisfaction. About the only fun they have from cat ownership is in having something live about the home, and in watching the cats eat. This is not enough, but unfortunately appears to be the extent of appreciation for many cat-owners.

For cats I am sorry because they are so neglected. Cats love to be trained, but there isn't one cat-owner in a million who realizes this. In fact, aside from psychologists, among all the thousands of cat-owners it has been my privilege to know, not a single one has ever really trained his or her cat.

As a matter of fact, most cats have trained their owners. When the cat meows before the refrigerator, the owner obediently opens the door and feeds the cat. When it meows at the back door, the owner is trained to let the cat out. He reacts to the cat's signals, something we shall discuss soon.

The reason for this neglect? I think it is because people do not know that a cat can be trained as easily as a dog, and by

Many hungry cats train their owners by meowing before the refrigerator.

almost the same methods. When I was a practicing veterinarian, I was struck by the interesting things which cats learned. When feeding time came around, every cat in the hospital—every one that had been there over three days, that is—would be standing rubbing its side against the cage front, meowing, with its tail erect. Fresh food and water were given. At the sound of dishes being put into other cages, the sound of food, we might say, all the cats behaved in this manner. After a few days, they invariably reacted to the sound of food and were actually responding or, as we say, being trained. This is precisely how other species behaved. If, at the sound of food, cats would rant back and forth, rubbing against the cage front and meowing, why wouldn't they behave as I wanted them to in response to other sounds or smells?

I tried some of these methods and the cats did respond. Why hadn't others tried too? There is a book about the mystery of the cat. The biggest mystery of all, and one not mentioned in that book is why no one has written a book until now telling cat-owners how to train their cats. From my experience, I can tell you there is nothing difficult about it. All you need to know are some of the basic principles of psychology and these are simply common sense.

Before we start discussing them, there are some interesting facts about cats which you should know if you are to get the most pleasure from cat ownership. I don't mean such mundane facts as how to feed or care for your cat, but some of the things scientists have discovered to make them more interesting to us.

Chapter Two

What You May Not Know About Cats

Search as one will through all the published studies of psychologists, one derives the distinct impression that cats have been studied less than any other common species of animal. We know vastly more about rats than we do about cats. Even raccoons and monkeys have been studied far more in proportion to their economic importance.

But patient psychologists have devoted many years to giving us such information as the following:

Cats are color blind. They can see only black and white shades, as we see an ordinary photograph. They can distinguish degrees of brightness clearly, however.

Cats can distinguish small forms and can differentiate between squares, triangles, and circles accurately.

They do not like uncommonly bright lights; they prefer shade or semi-darkness.

They get more pleasure from eating and drinking than from any other acts in life, so says a scientist after making over two hundred experiments to test their reactions.

Unlike puppies, each kitten has its own teat on the mother's belly and does not change from one to another.

Many cats nurse their young until and after full growth. It is not unusual to see a grandma cat nursing her grown kitten which in turn is nursing her kittens. But Grandma refuses to nurse her grandkittens.

From birth until three weeks of age, the mother cat initiates suckling by the kittens. From three to six weeks of age either the mother or the kittens initiate suckling. After six weeks it is up to the kittens. Cats do not produce milk until the kittens begin to nurse; then the mother manufactures it during the nursing process. (This is so with all species, even cattle.)

Cats vary greatly in their abilities to solve problems. There are some much "smarter" than others. The term "dumb cat" is not without a basis in fact. In some of the studies, there were some cats almost incapable of learning to do things which other cats learned quickly.

Cats learn a little watching other cats learning, but their ability in this respect is very limited.

Sleeping cats probably dream, as may be deduced by watching their eyes, ears, vibrissae and leg muscles twitch.

You have heard of the cat's whiskers. The real name is vibrissae. And few persons understand what an important organ of touch they are. Everyone knows that a cat measures the size of an opening it can crawl through by the vibrissae. And everyone is wrong because most cats can negotiate much smaller openings than the whiskers measure. These hairs are almost like radio antennae; they receive impressions of objects ahead so clearly that blind cats can get about without colliding provided the vibrissae are intact. But cut them off and the cats are almost helpless.

Cats can stand considerable rain and some love to go out and get wet. Some cats do their best mousing on rainy nights. Do cats instinctively kill and eat wild mice and rats? This instinct has seemed to intrigue many psychologists, and there have been some excellent published observations. You may have read that if kittens are raised with white rats, they will always be kind to rats. This, however, applies only to the rats with which they were raised. One explanation for it is that both come to smell more or less alike, the rat acquiring some of the cat's odor. When kittens are raised to maturity in isolation, about half will kill rats and mice without any learning.

When cats are raised in a rat-killing environment such as a barn, before the kittens are four months old, most of them are killing rats or mice of the kind they had seen their mothers kill, and some kill all kinds.

Grown, hungry cats behave very differently toward strange rats. They will eat baby rats and gray rats but, as I said, not white rats if they were raised with white rats. However they will eat white rats which have been shaved.

If cats are non-killers and are kept with cats that are killers, the non-killers soon become killers just from watching the others.

The more kittens are handled during the first month of life, the more precocious they are. Kittens left entirely alone are less likely to be as satisfactory pets when they are grown.

Cats do not have territories as many other species have. Song birds have their territories and sing to tell other birds of their species to keep away. Dogs have their territories which they protect when able to do so. Cats, on the other hand, roam everywhere.

Cats and dogs seem to supplement each other's wants in neighborhoods. The flight instinct of cats is stimulated by dogs, and the chasing instinct of dogs by cats. Each gets certain enjoyment from the presence of the other.

Cats and dogs, though natural antagonists, develop mutual tolerance for one another; even wild cats and dogs do so in time. Both are natural predators, the cat of rodents and birds, the dog of the same and larger species including the cat. But when they find they must tolerate one another through propinquity, they adjust nicely.

Not only does a cat's pulse rate increase when it becomes emotionally excited by a dog's barking; the red corpuscle count in the blood increases markedly.

When one cat among a group becomes the dominant individual, there is no fighting. But put the dominant cat in another group which has also sorted out itself in order of dominance and you will surely have a fight on your hands. In this respect, cats are reminiscent of groups of boys (or even adults).

Cats can localize the origin of a sound far better than human beings.

Not all white, blue-eyed, or pink-eyed cats are deaf, despite the commonly held opinion. But some yellow-eyed white cats are. Before any cat-owner condemns a cat for being stupid, he or she should be sure the cat can hear.

Some students believe they have detected extrasensory perception in cats.

Cats have three types of vocalizing: (1) murmurs or sounds made with closed mouths (purring): (2) basic vowel sounds starting with the mouth open and gradually becoming closed: (3) sounds made with the mouth held open in one position. Cats may seem to talk because the sounds vary in intensity. They definitely can make their wants known.

Cats are more repetitious than many other species. In escaping from puzzle boxes in laboratory studies, once a cat learns that by touching a certain lever it can escape, it constantly repeats this movement, rather than attempt to use other levers. The cat's learning is the acquisition of new signals (which we shall consider in detail later) for action by associating signal and act.

Cats love to pull strings, even shoelaces and yarn, which can be used as the basis of ingenious experiments and tricks. Why don't cat-owners arrange cat doorbells with strings for the cat to pull when it wants to come in?

In a crude way, cats can exhibit some foresight, and they have good memories.

Cats can be taught to be highly competitive. They will race for a goal such as food. Who ever heard of a cat race? But it might be fun. Imagine ten cats racing after a stuffed mouse around a fifty-yard track, like so many greyhounds pursuing a stuffed rabbit!

Cats can be highly stimulated to sexual activity by sounding the note *mi* of the fourth octave. By use of the same sound, kittens, before puberty, can be easily made to defecate, but after puberty the sound loses its powers of bowel stimulation and instead becomes a powerful genital excitant.

Cats under conditions of weightlessness are unable to right themselves, and thus float about in any position. A man can right himself by visual cues, but a cat cannot.

Cats can be made insane in much the same ways as human beings can.

A neurotic cat exhibits its neurosis by chronic anxiety, which it manifests by restlessness, trembling, crouching, and hiding: it is easily startled, and its pulse and respiration are disturbed. The latter are not likely to be observed. Because a cat exhibits these actions does not necessarily mean it is neurotic, however; it may be frightened in a new environment. The neurotic cat does not recover quickly from its neurosis as a frightened animal will.

Neurotic cats do not want to be handled. Hungry neurotics become more refractive if one pushes them to the food container. Even making the animal fast for longer intervals and increasing the hunger drive does not help overcome neurosis.

Cats may be made alcoholic. Alcohol will disorganize newly learned response patterns (another point we shall consider later). Neurotic cats will often seek alcoholic drinks which they have learned will ameliorate their neuroses.

The ability of cats to discriminate odors and tastes is probably similar to the order of human ability, which is probably just as well, especially for those living in human civilizations. Compared with dogs in these respects cats hardly recognize odors that to dogs are powerful.

Cats are one of the species of animals which do not ovulate unless they copulate. Separation after copulating is very painful for the catta because the male's penis has many barbs on it, much like a thistle. When he withdraws it from the vagina, he scratches the vaginal lining. It is probably this irritation which induces ovulation.

A catta comes in heat several times a year. If she does not copulate, she goes out of heat and shortly comes in again and again.

A dog with rabies will make its condition evident, by its actions, especially its boldness, but a rabid cat will usually go off and hide. It will attack other animals at times. It may bite cows in barns or may hide under a sofa and attack the ankle of a person who sits on it.

Chapter Three

The Natural Method
of Training Cats

What is the natural method of training? Before we get into that, we should discuss the ordinary methods of training animals. All of them are based upon the "force system." We force the animal to do something, and as we do, we make the doing of it somewhat pleasant. We talk about rewards and punishments. If we force the cat to lie down by pressing on it and saying *lie down* at the same time, we can in time accomplish the result we want. But there is a better way—an easier and quicker way.

The force system has been working for generations for trainers who have applied it to many species, but I predict that from now on, it will be considered passé. The acquisition of scientific knowledge of psychology is rapidly pushing it into the background.

Instead of using the force system, we are going to work with the cat's native instincts and teach it in much the same way that it learns by itself in nature. First, we are going to find out what the cat's innate needs and drives are, and then we are going to help it to fulfill those needs and drives and train it along the way. I say train when what I should say is *condition*.

Don't let the words *condition* or *conditioning* frighten you. This is not a book on animal psychology. It is just a simple book on how to train a cat by the natural method. No doubt, psychologists have used the natural method many times to train cats to perform various feats that we might call tricks, but I have never read a book wherein these principles have been applied to training cats for the benefit of their owners, for you or for me.

I realize that you could take a course in animal psychology, but if you did, you would have to learn a great many more terms and definitions that I am going to tell you about. In my day, I have trained hundreds of dogs for various tasks—from man-trailing to doing simple tricks. I originally used the old force method until I learned the up-to-date methods by study and application of them. I wrote a book, *The Natural Method of Dog Training*, which the public seems to have appreciated, and now we are applying the same principles to cats. I find they work just as well and indeed in the same way. I think you will really benefit if you study these simple principles until you have mastered their use. I strongly advise that you not attempt to train your cat until you do understand the principles fairly well.

Let me tell you now about the cats that are used in the illustrations throughout the book. I could have used magnificent longhairs, or Manx, or Siamese, or some other exotic breeds, but I chose these simple, plain old alley cats because they are representative of probably 95 per cent of all the cats in America. It is unnecessary to tell you that they learned to make all the responses which we wanted from them. You can see that in the photographs of them during their learning process, and you can observe the finished product. You can accomplish all of these things with your cat, too. Once you get the hang of it, you can do it just as easily as we did.

Your cat will have a distinct advantage over ours because she already understands her environment, whereas we took our cats into a new and unfamiliar environment.

Please don't tell me that your cat is too independent to be trained. Everybody, as I have said, thinks that about a cat, but many persons also think that about their dogs. When I used to ask my clients why they didn't train their cats, they invariably said, "Because my cat is too independent." When you apply the methods that you are going to learn in this book you will find that no cat is too independent to be trained.

The pictures in this book were taken in a room of our home where there was space against a wall to place a table six feet long and three feet wide. This is much larger than you need to use on which to train your cat. A two-by-three-foot table is really ample.

First I covered the wall with a beige blanket, thumb-tacked in place to make a background. For some of the lessons I covered the wall and table with maroon cloth. There was no pretense to fanciness. I wanted to make the layout as homey and as simple as possible and as nearly like what you could arrange at home, except that you don't need a background because you won't be taking pictures.

At first I placed a small rug on the table but found it slipped and caused the cats some anxiety so I substituted the larger piece of carpeting, which didn't slip. This is a point to remember in arranging your training table. If the carpet slips, and if you don't mind holes in the table, then tack it down. This I couldn't do, because the table I used is an antique.

While I was conditioning the cats to respond in various ways, the photographer was snapping the pictures. Each lesson took about fifteen minutes. When you condition your cat by the natural method you will acquire greater competency with each lesson and with each newly learned accomplishment by the cat you'll find it is a little easier to have her learn the next.

Chapter Four

Rapport

There is one principle which every good animal trainer understands, namely that he should have *rapport* with his subject. The
word rapport is particularly applicable here; it means a harmonious
and sympathetic relationship. It means that you and your cat
get along well and that both of you understand and appreciate
your rightful positions.

How are you going to establish rapport if you haven't already
done so? In the event that you have some understanding about
the proper relationship of dog-owner to his dog, you must
not let this interfere with the knowledge of relationship of cat-
owner to cat. Dogs travel in packs like wolves, and there is
always a pack leader who has won that position through his
dominance and fighting ability. Cats do not travel in packs like
dogs, but they do, when kept in packs together, as you read
previously, work out the order of dominance. I have known
many cats that completely dominated their owners, who virtually
became slaves to them. This is not proper rapport. You must be
the dominant one in your companionship with the cat and the

cat must learn early to understand it. If the cat fights you, then she is dominant. You will then have to be so firm with the animal that she comes to understand that *you* are dominant.

Not that you can't use these methods to train the cat without first having established rapport. You can but you can train her better if you establish the proper relationship. To establish rapport you simply have to be around the cat for a time until it comes to know that you are its friend. Dogs love to share your activities. Cats are sufficiently independent so that they want to do things on their own and by themselves, but they're not too independent to be taught.

Whatever your cat does when she is around you, she does to please herself, not because she loves to please *you*. The same is true of dogs. The dog loves to please himself and so does the cat, and this is a good thing to know because we can use it in our training.

One of the interesting facts you will find as you train your cat is that the person who feeds it is not the one to whom it will show the most deference but the person who trains it: that will be you. That is the best way to establish rapport—to work with the animal. So with this little bit of understanding between us, let's have a look at the theories which underlie the natural method of training. Perhaps I should not have used the word *theory*, and I wouldn't have, except perhaps sometime in the future these ideas may be changed. They are really facts as we understand them at present.

The first fact to remember is that *your cat's behavior is never uncaused*. She never even purrs, twitches her whiskers, turns her head, lies down, moves her tail, stretches, meows, or does anything else unless there is a cause for it. With her it is all cause and effect.

There are countless reasons why your cat acts the way she does. If she tastes bitter food, she spits it out; if she hears a noise, she responds by raising her ears and appearing alert. If she feels excessive heat, she draws away from it; if you scratch her back just in front of her tail, she will raise her hind end up high or else squat. If she hears a dog bark, her hair may stand up along her back; if she smells something she likes, her mouth will water.

Let's have this understanding, too: your cat does not think as you do. I realize that many people hold an opposite opinion, but so far as psychologists can determine, they are wrong and if you are able to demonstrate that your cat really thinks, believe me, all psychologists would like to know about it. As yet, no one has been able to demonstrate such an activity under controlled scientific conditions.

Each of the movements which I have mentioned, is a demonstration of a *reflex*. You and I and our cats are simply a collection of reflexes which have been conditioned, and, as kittens grow up, new reflexes can be demonstrated. At first, the kitten's reflexes are few and simple. In the beginning she is blind and deaf. When she smells the odor of one of her mother's teats, she nuzzles one and opens her mouth, and when the tongue wraps around the teat, she sucks. When the milk runs into the back of her mouth, she swallows. When her stomach feels full, she stops feeding.

When the kitten is cold, she cries, and as she grows older, she cries when she is lonesome. When she is hurt, she screams. She never has to be taught to climb a tree to escape a dog or to do countless other things which are inherited as instincts.

What is a reflex? It is defined as an *"involuntary, invariable, adaptive response to a stimulus."* This definition takes some explaining. Everyone knows that when a bright light shines in our own or an animal's eyes, the pupil contracts. This is a reflex. The light is a stimulus. When the doctor taps you on the knee with a rubber hammer, your foot flies forward. That is another reflex—a very simple reflex, as is the contraction of the pupil of your eye. The eye pupil always contracts when a bright light strikes it. The action is *invariable*. The *response* is the reaction to the stimulus or the constricting of the pupil. Now what do we mean by the word *adaptive*? It simply means that the reflexes with which we are born and those which we develop as we grow older are there to help us survive and reproduce. If we couldn't adapt, we would perish as a species, and so would cats.

I'm sure that you have heard the term *conditioned reflex,* but let me explain it in case you do not know precisely what it is. Suppose you and I sit on opposite sides of a table. Between us is an electric light. We darken the room. Naturally, the pupils of our eyes will enlarge—dilate. That is a simple reflex over which we have no control.

Now I press a button and light the bulb. What happens? Our pupils contract. This is an invariable, uncontrollable reflex, and the light is the stimulus.

But suppose I press a button, light the bulb, and I also say *contract.* You hear the word—this word accompanies the *stimulus.* We go through the exercise flicking the light off and on in the room thirty or forty times and every time the bulb lights, you hear the word contract. What will have happened to you? You will have to some degree, become conditioned. I can meet you two weeks later on a dark day when your pupils are partially dilated and I can say the word to you, *contract,* and your pupils will contract. I have you in my power to that extent.

Are you beginning to see the difference between the force system of training and the natural system? This is the first step to understanding. We are going to condition the cat's reflexes.

How do we do it?

First, we ask ourselves, *What are the cat's needs?* She has many needs, so let's discuss some of them.

Chapter Five

Some Ordinary Needs

In a nutshell, what we are going to do in training *your* cat and ours (which process you will see described in the workshop chapters) is simply to couple one of the needs of the cat with an effective method of conditioning his or her reflexes. In this way we shall accomplish education.

Need for Companionship

We frequently read or hear it said that a cat loves companionship. This I doubt very much, because I think most cats are loners. They never hunt in packs but are completely independent. The only reason they like you or me as company is for what they can get from us, usually food or scratching. As I have already pointed out, a cat doesn't love to please us any more than a dog does, even though both are said to respond to our commands because they love to please.

No doubt they do become lonesome, but in a very self-sufficient way. There's your cat sitting contentedly on the window sill. She sees you walking up the path to the house. Or if you live in an apartment, she hears your key in the lock. In either case the cat is there at the door to meet you, purring and rubbing against your leg. She seems to be welcoming you. But is she? She is exhibiting a habit—a conditioning—which slowly developed by your having done something to her or for her which she found pleasant. You had filled one of her needs. Scratched her ears, fed her, let her out to relieve herself? Yes, relieving herself is also filling a need.

Contrast this behavior of apparently welcoming you with that of several cats in my large cat colony. There were some which got into the playful habit of knocking the water containers off their hooks and wetting their cage bottoms. My assistant, I learned later, when he found the water spilled, replaced the container and at the same time slapped the cat. Later, when he no longer was taking care of the cats, every one of those smart cats which got slapped still shied away from us when we opened the cage doors—even as long as *six months after* the slapping stopped. And this despite the fact that we took special pains to gentle those cats by scratching their ears and backs. In their cases, the close presence of a human being was a signal for avoidance. But in the case of your cat, your presence is a signal of something pleasant. Of course your cat comes to meet you. Of course she shows her pleasure by purring.

Any cat can be conditioned to respond to kindness. I have in mind my favorite cat in the colony. This was a completely feral cat—caught in a Havahart trap in the woods to prevent its eating the squirrels which a neighbor had for his pets. The cat learned that the squirrels were tame, and she would cleverly hide behind a stone wall and catch squirrel after squirrel. Finally she was trapped. What a fierce, snarling beast she was while in that trap! I needed a cat to replace an unsatisfactory one in my colony, so I took this furious thing to see if I could gentle her. First she went into quarantine where she was studied, because it would have been tragic to bring any disease into the colony. We learned that she was heavily infested with the rabbit-host form of tapeworm, which demonstrated that she must have lived partly on rabbits.

But how to deworm her! I decided to tranquilize her and then gave the pill which removed the worms.

To handle her in transferring her to the nutrition laboratory, I dropped a many-folded blanket over her and got her into her permanent cage. She was in quarantine six days before she touched any food. In the colony she ate at night. If I put my hand into the cage she flew at it (most strange cats retreat into a corner) and would bite. But after a week, my presence and my hand became a signal that food was coming; it was a signal for filling a want. By the end of two weeks I could touch her with my fist, but she would scratch if my fingers were extended. I rubbed my knuckles against her ears and finally scratched her head until she tolerated my action, and now when I rub her head, she gently reaches out a paw and signals me to come back and scratch her more. She has become a completely docile cat who enjoys being picked up; one would never know she had once been feral.

The Need to Be Scratched

In the case of this cat I used scratching for mild conditioning, and in her case it worked just as well as if I have given her food as a reinforcement. Finally when she would put one paw on top of my hand and I would at once scratch her ear, I began to say *Shake* just as she put out her paw and she had her ear scratched immediately. After a while I could put my hand in and say *Shake* and she was conditioned in a short time so that now she responds perfectly to the word *Shake* without having her ear scratched. All cats love to be scratched on the back in front of the tail and will, as mentioned previously, usually raise their whole hind end.

Need to Escape

Cats kept in small quarters like to get out where they can visit in the neighborhood. The curious fact is that if they are raised in a small area—say in a small cage—from kittenhood they never show any desire to escape. Only the cats which have already

Cats so enjoy being scratched that scratching can be used as a reinforcement.

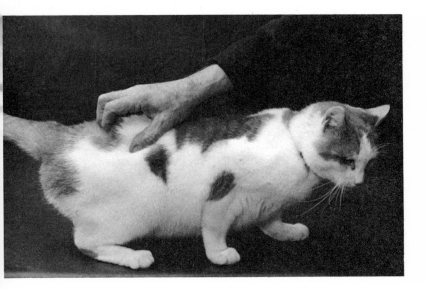

Stroking the cat's head and ears is also enjoyable to most cats.

learned about the neighborhood want to escape when confined in small quarters. One of my cats learned very quickly that it could open the latch and escape. Of course, it monkeyed around with the latch until it found that it opened, but after that this trial-and-error kind of learning had become part of its education. It would escape very quickly until an additional latch was put on the cage door.

Hunger

It is a fact that a hungry cat can be conditioned by anyone who is patient and sympathetic, but when it is handled by a person it knows, the early results are better. Rapport will come much more quickly even with a stranger who is working with the cat than it does between the cat and owner who behaves toward his or her pet as most pet owners do.

Here we must consider the question of hunger because it is

this convenient and simple need that we shall use. So few Americans have ever experienced true hunger that most persons have weird ideas about it. As I know so well from my veterinary experience in working with pet owners, trying to get them to reduce overfat animals, most of them think that hunger is painful and that hunger must be appeased or the pet will promptly die.

In a wild state most animals live a feast-or-famine existence. Why do you think animals get fat? Ever stop to think about it? Obviously it is because during their evolution, those which possessed the greatest ability to store up the surplus food they ate in the form of body fat could weather a long period of a complete lack of food and live on their accumulated nourishment they carried with them. Which means that our cats' ancestors, and now our cats, can live for long periods of time on the stored fat. A few days with nothing to eat is trivial. Cats accidentally left in houses without food have been found in good health, if thin, more than a month later. For water they lick condensation from water pipes. Without water, however, a cat will die in less than two weeks.

Knowing that fasting is painless, psychologists prepare animals for conditioning by putting them on low-calorie diets until they have lost about a quarter of their normal weight. When this is done, the animals are always so greedily hungry that they will respond to tidbits every day until they reach normal weight.

Once when I was planning to do some hunting and didn't want to tire myself carrying surplus weight, I lopped off 47 pounds in sixty days. My normal weight at six feet is about 175–180, but I stopped at 167. Every year in the fall I took off 25 to 35 pounds and experienced no pain in the process. And this was before the low-carbohydrate diet, which permits us to eat but not feel hungry as we lose our surplus. I'm sure that with my lost weight I would have made an excellent subject for psychological research if hunger had been used as a conditioner.

So don't feel any qualms at knowing your cat is a little hungry. Try fasting for thirty-six hours and you will experience no pain. *Thirty-six hours!* A cat fed once a day eats every twenty-four hours. Letting the cat go another twelve hours seems to produce the best results. A twenty-four-hour hungry cat will not work for us as well as a thirty-six-hour hungry cat. And strangely enough, one fasted for forty-eight hours is not quite as keen as one fasted thirty-six hours.

If your cat is used to drinking milk, she will have to drink water. Do not let her go out. If she is permitted to go out she may catch field mice, moles, birds, grasshoppers, or other kinds of food. And of course she may visit kind-hearted neighbors.

No, when you begin to condition your cat, there can be no putting the cat out for the night as many cat-owners do. The results will more than justify your use of will power.

What does your cat love to eat? Can you think of any item that she will greedily take from your fingers? Perhaps not, because your cat may never have been sufficiently hungry. A reinforcing tidbit must be something the cat likes.

The way all the loose neighborhood cats used to surround the fish peddler one would think that fish was their prime delicacy. The odor of fish does attract cats, but the flavor is often less well appreciated than some other foods. Moreover cats vary greatly in their food preferences. Some prefer brewer's yeast tablets to any other tidbit. Some like chicken or turkey. In studies made on taste, it was learned that all the distinctive flavor of meats resides in the fat. When all fat is removed a cat or a human being cannot distinguish pork from veal or beef. Cooking greatly enhances flavor—for cats as well as for us.

Here are some *dont's* which should be helpful to you as you condition your cat:

Don't start unless she is hungry—thirty-six hours hungry. There won't be any want to be fulfilled if she is not hungry.

Don't lose your patience.

Don't delay an instant in giving the reinforcement. Even seconds is too long. If your cat can be reinforced while in the act of responding it would be even better, but since that can't be done, the next best thing is to have the reinforcement right there as the response is completed.

Don't try to force a cat into action. This is why nearly everyone believes that cats cannot be trained.

Don't stop your conditioning at the time you see you are successful. You are training the cat to jump onto a chair. She responds to your signal unerringly five times, at this point you have only taught her to respond to the signal, you have not truly conditioned her. To do that you must have her repeat the response at least twenty times at the first session. Then twenty more times at the next session.

Don't try forcing, pulling, pushing. At first you may be using the light leash. Your natural inclination is to give the cat an assist by pulling on it, or you may show her what you want her to do, perhaps by lifting her. No, don't! That is the old method long discarded by psychologists.

Don't try to train a sick cat. By sick, I mean a cat with any ailment. Ear mites and skin diseases drive a cat to scratch. A collar and leash on a cat with ear mites will probably hurt her because pressure on the ear canals is exerted by any forward pull of the

Instead, fulfill a want (hunger in this case), reinforcing the cat's action instantly with a tidbit as he responds to a signal.

leash. An ear-mite-infested cat will sit down and scratch violently. Should you attempt to establish rapport with her, you can't do it in the usual manner, by scratching her ears.

A cat with tartar-coated, odorous teeth is not a fit subject for training because she cannot savor her food as well as one with clean teeth. A cat with loose teeth is an even less trainable pupil. Have any loose teeth and tartar removed if necessary.

Internal parasites cause anemia and loss of condition. You need a keen cat to work with. If your cat is sluggish and lacks appetite, have a fecal examination made by your veterinarian and if she is infested have her dewormed.

External parasites—lice and fleas—plague a cat or cause anemia. Rid her of them so that she can focus all of her attention on her lessons.

Don't work with your cat until you have cut her nails. There are some cats, only a small percentage, if my experience is any criterion, which will hook their claws into one's hand. Most cats scrupulously avoid doing so. They may extend their claws right up to the point of trying to take something from your fingers but stop short of using them. Any hungry cat may try to hook onto some passing food and if your finger is in the way unintentionally give you a dig.

It is well to keep every house cat's claws trimmed; a pair of ordinary nail clippers suffices as the tool. Simply press the foot from top to bottom and the claws will stick out. Cut only the transparent part, which is horn without nerves or blood vessels. This may protect some furniture, too.

Chapter Six

Using Signals

Cats have the five senses: taste, smell, hearing, feeling, seeing. But they have other senses as well, the sense of balance, for example. In order to condition the cat thoroughly what sound or smell, or what object can we use best to couple with the incentive (food) that we're going to use in our training? Anything that gets through to one of the five senses could be used. Why not a sound? We are all conditioned to sounds—words—which elicit from us certain actions or thoughts. Let's choose a sound which we will make that the cat will couple with the reflex that we're going to condition. Cats have remarkable hearing. What would be easiest for you to use in this instance? A toot on a whistle? A snapping of the fingers? The noise made by a "cricket" such as children buy in the dime store, which makes a little click-click sound? Or perhaps a sound which to you or me is a word but is nothing but a sound to the cat? I prefer words, because then we can use a different one for each trick we're going to teach our cat to perform.

Should you make the sound loudly or softly? Since a cat hears well, it is much better to condition a cat with softly spoken words.

If you start with loud words you must always use them. Calculate in advance how loud you are going to speak, and stick to that level of sound.

It is also well to have a sound which is in the nature of an alert. You might use the cat's name for the sound. Most cats must think their name is "Pussy" because most everyone says, "Here, Pussy," when they talk to them.

Chapter Seven

Reinforcements

Kinds to Try

Now, a few words about the kind of tidbits to use. It may surprise you as it did me to discover that small slices of chicken are not the most appealing foods you can use. I asked many cat lovers, persons with years of experience with many cats, what tidbits the cats would love best. Some frankly said their opinions would be guesses; all the rest said chicken. But that was not what I found.

Chicken in small slices will do for a hungry cat—do, that is, if you have nothing better, but small slices of roast beef or corned beef are better appreciated. I tried small sardines but found them too messy to use, the oil from them dripping on floor or table. When laid on absorbent paper and rolled they proved efficient. The size piece was one third of a sardine. My cats liked the big Maine or Japanese sardines, those packed in tomato sauce, better than the Norwegian kind. They shred up so easily that they must be cut with a sharp knife.

One of my cats worked well on pieces of yeast tablets but for the others it was not as efficient as beef. Your cat may have a special liking for some food—cheese perhaps, or boiled liver. Use whatever it finds most palatable.

Amount to Give

The average cat needs about two ounces of food a day, figured on dry weight. Meats have about 60 per cent water, so the total amount of beef needed would be five ounces: of canned cat food, eight ounces: of sardines, five ounces. When your cat is thirty-six-hours hungry and needs about seven or eight ounces of meat to make up for the half-day she was not fed, in addition to today's ration, for the tidbit reinforcements use half that amount, three or four ounces cut into small pieces. That will be enough for all the responses you want in one conditioning session.

When the training session has been completed, give all the remainder of the ration as you usually feed it. You may be feeding a canned or a dry food. Give half the usual amount, because she will have consumed half of her daily food requirement in the form of reinforcements.

We start with a dozen tidbits of something that our cat likes very much and also with a cat that is thirty-six-hours hungry. But where shall we have the cat? How about right in the living room? On the floor just beside your chair you have a small food pan. Take a tidbit from the jar, or wherever you have them concealed. Let the cat smell it and drop it in the pan and say "Bess," if that is your cat's name. Now, wait a few moments after she has eaten it and wandered away a little distance. Say "Bess" again and let her see you drop the tidbit in the pan. Keep repeating this and gradually she will come to associate the word "Bess" with food in the pan and coming to get it. This will be an attention-getter. When you are thoroughly satisfied that she knows that the word "Bess" means to come to you and eat the tidbit from the pan, you can start conditioning her with some other response.

Now actually, if you were trying to condition her thoroughly to the word "Bess" and the response to come to you and get the tidbit, you should do it at least twenty times. Let two days go by, and after she has fasted thirty-six hours, do it twenty more times. By that time she won't be able to resist when she hears the word "Bess." However, this is not going to be necessary in the present case, because we're going to use the word "Bess" every time when we are conditioning, as an attention-getter, and so it will save a lot of time if we just start her off this way and each time in the future use the word "Bess" before we sound the signal.

I think we should understand thoroughly what the idea of a reinforcement is. Some people call the tidbit that the animal gets, a reward. I think this is a mistake. The animal is not working for a reward. What it is doing is gradually having its want fulfilled. In other words, the fulfillment of the need is done by reinforcing. Each time a correct response is made the cat's need is slowly satisfied. I like to think of it in the same way that one thinks about a sailboat sailing on a lake. The sail is set at an angle to the wind. Not one great puff of wind sends the boat to its destination but constant small puffs which strike the sail and bounce off, one after the other, in a steady stream. Each puff is a reinforcement, and the boat moves ahead.

Now, how large should our reinforcements be? I find it advisable to calculate what the total caloric needs for the cat would be for one day. I divide this in half and then I divide that portion into twenty individual tidbits. At each lesson I plan at least twenty responses and have one tidbit or reinforcement for each correct response.

Next we have to know how soon after the response to the signal the tidbit or reinforcement should be given.

Think of a cat burning itself on a hot stove. It feels the heat as it approaches, which you might say is a signal. It touches the hot stove and *instantly* feels the pain. But suppose that it felt the heat, then touched the stove but felt no pain for a minute or two after having touched it. Would the cat have become conditioned? Indeed not! The ideal way to present the reinforcement is instantaneously. Even five seconds delay cuts down on the efficiency, and this is especially true in the early conditioning sequences.

REINFORCING: *Our pupil must have his tidbit the instant he responds properly.*

What about repetition? How much repetition is really necessary? To get the proper response, sometimes only a very few repetitions are necessary, but that doesn't mean that the animal is properly conditioned. What we try to do when we condition the animal or the cat is to have conditioning as nearly permanent as possible. From a practical point of view, it works well to repeat each response twenty times and then skip two days. You may be astonished to find that all the energy that you expended in the first day seems to be wasted. But it is not. After about three or four responses, the cat will be far ahead, and by the end of the session it will be conditioned well enough so that it will remember the conditioning for a matter of several weeks.

Having learned it, it's necessary that we exercise the cat in the response to our signals occasionally in order to keep them from fading—becoming forgotten.

All this time we've been talking about positive conditioning. And here it seems appropriate to discuss briefly the term *brainwashing*. It is appropriate particularly now since we hear the word so wrongly used by people who should be better informed. Repeatedly one hears persons say that someone has been brainwashed when what that person means is that the person has been conditioned. Brainwashing means losing the conditioning. We'll have more about this later. There are several ways of bringing it about. One of those ways is simply not using the responses to a stimulus. Please keep this in mind and remember to exercise your cat in repetitions of the response to the stimulus which it has learned. Otherwise, the cat will become brainwashed.

We should also consider the question of *where* you can get best results in training your cat. I tried several places, all the way from letting the cat go into any room it chose in the house down to the training of the cat on the table. I tried using no leash at all and using a leash. I strongly recommend training on a leash and also training on a table. You can train on a table with yourself standing before it and you can train sitting in a chair.

If you decide to use a table, and leash, better put a hook in the wall behind the table about six inches above the top. Use as light a leash as possible. If your cat is not accustomed to a collar, put one on a few days before you expect to begin your educating. If the cat objects to the leash, try accustoming her to both collar and leash, right on the table top where you will conduct your school. If you have to leave the cat, she will probably chew through the leash. Better use a light chain or a leash made of a limber piece of thin wire cable. Pet stores sell these cable leashes covered with plastic. They are entirely satisfactory. Once a cat learns she can chew through a leash, instead of paying attention to you, she may annoy you by constantly chewing on it.

Of course, the place of training depends a great deal on what you want your cat to do. There are some responses that cannot be made on a table. I told one deaf woman how to condition her cat to let her know when the doorbell rang. This was quickly done with the help of a person with normal hearing. What we shall do in the workshop chapter which follows is to show you how to train your cat to execute a variety of responses, none of which may be of value to you but each one is illustrative and you will see that when you condition your own cat that the same principles hold throughout. Later on we shall discuss negative conditioning which will help you to break your cat of some objectionable practices if she happens to have any.

In some parts of the world, the dog-owners have established rules in training. One of the basic rules is that no dog may be trained by the use of food. Of course, the people who make such rules know practically nothing about dog psychology or they wouldn't have agreed on such nonsense. In one of the books which I have, telling why this rule was put into effect, it states that the dog is not a seal.

If you have seen animal trainers with seals, you know how very effectively seals can be conditioned by the use of fish. For each response the seal is given instantly either a piece of fish or a small fish. Actually this is a model of proper conditioning. For all we know seals may be much more intelligent animals than dogs.

I mention this because you may have heard about this dog

"formula" and think that it applies to your cat, namely that you must not train a cat by using food. Actually very few cats in the world have ever been trained at all. As I have said, most of them have trained their owners. Because of their independent temperaments cats are very difficult to train simply by the use of kind words or petting or having their ears scratched. But as you will see, it is not at all difficult to condition a cat to respond properly to stimuli provided the proper reinforcements are used.

Your cat is not a seal. Before you are finished conditioning your cat to the proper responses, you may wish that it was more like a seal in its quick ability to learn and ability to execute such remarkable feats as seals perform.

We come to another consideration, namely, what kind of cat should one undertake to train? Well, almost no one will train a tomcat because tomcats do not make very good house pets. This is because of the odor they emit when they urinate. Shall we condition a neutered tomcat? By all means. That is as easy as conditioning a neutered catta.

My advice to you is not to try to work with a female that has not been neutered unless you are sure that she is not going to be in heat at the times when you are planning to do your work. The urge to mate seems to be overpowering, and a catta in heat will roll around and assume a mating attitude and frequently cry out. If you must train a catta, wait until she is over her heat period before you work with her. Then, to call your attention to what I said in the second chapter, unless she mates she will go out of heat only to come in again in a very short time. So you may have just got started when you have to postpone your training for another few days or a week until she again goes out of this phase.

So, with the foregoing in our memory, let us proceed to do what almost everyone believes can't be done—train a cat. We shall train our cats, and you will then train your own in the very same way.

Chapter Eight

Workshop

To accomplish our conditioning, we need a place as free as possible from distractions. Since each session will require about a half hour, choose a time when you expect the fewest interruptions. It is most disconcerting to have a friend drop in or the grocer deliver an order or the man come to read a meter, or the children return from school when conditioning is going on. You may find that late evening is the best time for you.

Nor need you be alone while the lessons are being taught, provided there is no coming and going of different persons. The cats whose pictures you see in this chapter had only two persons working with them—a photographer and myself. The cats learned not even to fear the flashbulbs. But once they became accustomed to us, the barking of a dog outside the house slowed their responses because they were unable to concentrate during the barking and for a short while after it had stopped. Being interrupted while I was called to the telephone did not disturb the cats; they went right to work again as soon as I returned. They were only upset by an intruder.

In the place you have chosen, which may be a vacant room, a garage, a corner of the cellar, you will find it easiest to have a cloth-covered table on which the cat will be conditioned. I strongly suggest that you not use the kitchen or dining room because, if you accustom your cat to working on a table in one of these rooms, you will surely find her jumping on your dining or kitchen table or onto cabinets and even the stove—places where she is definitely *persona non grata*. Indeed, it will require some negative conditioning to insure that she knows these are places where she is unwelcome.

Why use a table at all? You really don't have to, you know. If you are comfortable sitting on the floor or bending over, the floor will do. But if you don't feel the need for deep-knee bends or other gyrations twenty or more times in succession, use a table; it is much easier on one's back and legs. A bare metal or wooden table will do, because cat's feet do not slip much, but my experience leads me to know that a cloth cover, into which the cat's nails can grip, even though ever so slightly, will add to the pupil's confidence.

A chair is useful too. One is sufficient. At first you can use it in teaching your cat to jump to the table via the chair. After that sit on it yourself. You may feel lazy for doing it, but puss won't mind.

Two other most important requirements have yet to be provided: tidbits and a signal. It is a good idea to feed the cat regularly on a dry cat food which is complete and wholesome and to use something more delectable for the tidbits. Now, please don't tell me, "My cat won't eat this or won't eat that," because you are wrong; she will eat it if it is wholesome. You only think she won't because you have never made her hungry enough to eat it. Remember that fasting is entirely painless. Any cat can fast for a week, with only water available, and remain as healthy as ever, perhaps more so.

As a veterinarian I have heard the old complaint, "My cat won't eat this, etc.," and surely several hundred times I have watched cats brought to be boarded or treated for some disease, refuse food for twenty-four hours and even for seventy-two. But after that they ate, and when they went home would eat what was set before them until, alas, they were again spoiled.

You know how the cat you are trying to unspoil comes to the refrigerator and yowls for food. Sort of sets you crazy, doesn't it? Well, that's the way you should prepare your cat for conditioning. You won't satisfy her with what she wants so badly all at once, but bit by bit, as she responds to the act you are conditioning her to do.

A cat on a leash seems abnormal to some owners, but, believe me, it is not. The leash can be most useful. True, cats don't like it, but they can soon be conditioned to like it. Some of my cats resented a collar and leash so I put a collar on a week before the training began and let them get the feel of it. At the start of conditioning, I applied the very light leash you see attached to the collar in the pictures. At first it was not used to lead cats but simply as an attachment. I wanted them to like it by associating it with something good to eat.

And now we were ready for our first lesson: *To jump onto a chair*. We needed a signal so we used the word *Chair*. It could have been a squeak, a bell, a cricket or what have you, but a word was simple and she knew its meaning, so we used that. From here on out, I shall not tell you how we did it, but how you should do it.

Lesson 1. To Jump onto a Chair

Bess is thirty-six-hours hungry. In a cellophane bag you have her tidbits—reinforcements. Let her walk around dragging her light leash. Give her one tidbit, which she will welcome, and she'll purr and perhaps rub against your leg, looking up at you for more. She's ready. Hold a tidbit over the chair seat and say *Chair*. She can't reach it when she stands on her hind legs but will soon jump up. Instantly, let her eat the tidbit. Lift her down. Repeat. After a few repetitions, if you are standing near the chair she will start jumping onto the seat without a command but always, as she does so say *Chair* and reinforce the action.

Now move away from the chair some distance and say *Chair*.
If she responds, step over and give her the tidbit, and move
farther away. Finally, you will be able to step outside of the
door and when Bess hears you say *Chair* she will jump up onto it.
Keep doing this until she has jumped up at least twenty times.
After that feed her as much of her dry food as she needs for her
day's ration.

As you lead her away from the training room, hold her leash,
and she will probably walk beside you, looking up for more
food. In this way she will have partially learned that a leash is
good and jumping on a chair is fun. And you will be having fun
too.

Whenever something reinforces any particular activity of a cat,
that reinforcement makes it more likely that the cat will repeat
what it was doing.

Illustration: Your cat happens to be standing before your refrigerator just as you take out a bottle of milk. She hears the door
click, sees you pour some milk into a pitcher and then pour
some into her bowl on the floor. You have reinforced her standing
before the refrigerator. After she repeats the action a few times,
just the click of opening the refrigerator door is her signal to come
and sit there. She can't help it.

I said that the cat cannot help responding. She can't, but her
response may not be instantaneous. And here is where the cat's
independence is exhibited. Unless she is quite hungry she may
look at you with an expression almost of defiance, which seems to
say, "when I get good and ready." This was displayed over and over
by one of my cats (Moxie) when I was conditioning him to jump
onto a chair. I thought, after a dozen responses that he knew
what to do, but just then, he held his tail erect and walked
about in front of the chair and refused to jump. After some
delay, he looked up and jumped without my having said *Chair*
—a delayed response. This action has been exhibited on several
occasions by Moxie.

Teach your cat to jump onto a chair at the word CHAIR.

Here is Moxie sitting awaiting another signal.

Lesson 2. *To Jump onto a Table*

Our signal can be *Table* or a clicking sound like the cricket made when he returned from his honeymoon. *Chh, chh,* made by your tongue against your teeth. Cats respond very well to that and can hear it when you do it quietly, so that friends don't notice it and wonder what makes your cat perform.

So two days after the first lesson we have Bess hungry and eager to get to work. Attach the leash and see if she objects to being led to the training area. If she does, let the leash drag. When I trained my cats, they had apparently learned during one lesson that the leash was good and made no objection when I pulled on it gently.

First, rehearse your Bess in her reaction to the signal *Chair*. She may not respond as well as you expect but that's par. After a couple of reminders she will have "caught on." Exercise her a dozen times and when she is on the chair seat with the chair pushed next to the table, say *Table* and hold her tidbit above the table top. She will jump up onto the table. When you take her down, place her on the chair seat, say *Table,* and repeat the exercise twenty times.

Now put her on the floor and say *Chair* and when she has jumped onto the chair say *Table*. She will jump up.

Next, see if she will jump from the table down to the chair at the signal. Probably she won't, because all of her action has been upward. But in a few minutes you can condition her to respond to the word *Chair* whether she jumps up or down.

At this same session, try her reaction to *Table* when the chair is pulled away. She will probably hop right up. My cats all did.

Lesson 3. *Chair, Table, Down*

This will be a combination of the responses learned in Lessons 1 and 2. It is necessary to do this in order to prevent confusion.

Pull the chair away from the table and say *Chair*. If she jumps onto the table she receives no tidbit and to that small extent the reaction is extinguished. But indicate the chair and she will respond.

Now say *Table*, and if she jumps on the chair she needs more conditioning. Pull the chair next to the table. Tell her *Table*, and after her action has been reinforced, say *Chair*. If you have to, entice her to jump down and reinforce when she has done as you want.

Now teach her *Down*, a most useful signal for any cat to understand. After she has responded to *Table* or *Chair* entice her if necessary by holding out the tidbit close to the floor. Instantly, as she jumps down, give it to her.

When she has jumped up on the table and *Down* to the floor a dozen times, reinforced for each correct response, try her on the chair. By then she will know you want her to jump down when you say *Down*.

So, you see, you have now conditioned her and made the rest of the training much easier for yourself. No longer need you pick Bess up and sit her on the table for future conditioning; she's ready and waiting to proceed. And notice this: every time she learns a new response, it seems that she learns the next one just a little more easily than the last. Part of this improvement you must chalk up to your own learning because you are catching on, becoming more proficient.

By now, can you see how much more efficient the natural method is over the old force method? Force doesn't work very well with cats, which may be the basic reason why almost everyone used to think that cats were too independent to be trained. But no cat is independent of her appetite.

Lesson 4. To Respond to a Call

One of the first responses you should expect in your cat is for her to come when you call her. This can be done in a short time or over a period of days. A good illustration of slow conditioning is the old custom of ringing the dinner bell to call farm hands in for meals. At least twice a day they heard it and walked to the

TABLE *is the signal to jump up, and quickly his action is reinforced.*

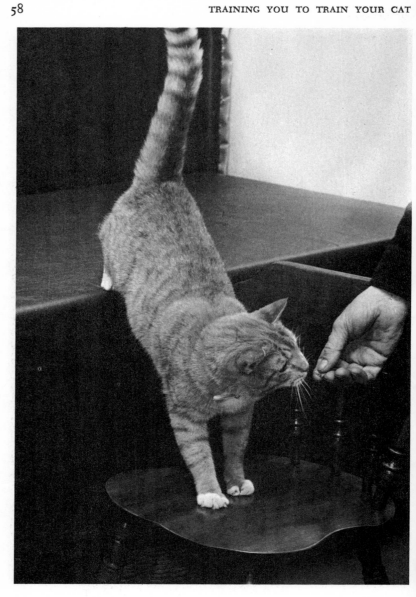

DOWN *comes to mean down. Moxie is given the tidbit just as he lands on the chair.*

Now he jumps down without seeing the tidbit. From here on, the word DOWN *means from any height on which the cat is standing.*

farmhouse and ate. After enough of these responses, a dinner bell ringing brought saliva into their mouths, figuratively and often literally.

You can feed your cat once or twice a day; as she smells food and comes to eat it, say, *Here, Kitty.* After some weeks she will have become so conditioned that you can call her when no food is in the offing.

Or you can let her go hungry for a while and then divide half of her daily ration into about twenty pieces and condition her. Conditioning is even better at two sessions, two days apart. Say *Here, Kitty* as she approaches her food dish, and drop a tidbit. Move away from it, and when she also moves away, go back and repeat. Do this over and over until the tidbits are gone, and then give her the remainder of her ration.

Go through it twenty more times two days later when she is again hungry, and after that, exercise her in the response to the call, every time she goes out or even around the house. Just some ear rubbing or back scratching is enough reinforcement from then on.

Lesson 5. To Jump onto a Chair on a Table

This time I'll show you how I conditioned Moxie. He is an altered yellow tiger cat. He clawed a man badly and the man gave him to me, but he has really been gentle since I have had him. Moxie loves to work at conditioning; he's a natural.

As in the case of all the cats, a little getting acquainted period was useful and consisted of ear rubbing, smoothing his coat, scratching his back, and conditioning him to jump onto the table, which he learned quickly. Of course one can bend over and lift any cat up but why not teach a response?

I wanted to teach him to jump onto a child's high chair on the table. The chair, incidentally is one in which my Whitney great-grandfather sat when he was a baby. In all, four generations of Whitneys have used it. Moxie didn't know he was the first cat to enjoy it!

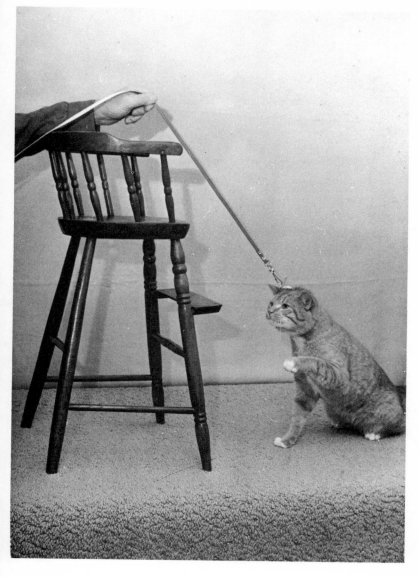

We don't try to force the cat to jump; it won't work.

*We coax him with a tidbit and sound the signal—*CHAIR—*as he responds—in this case be standing close to the high chair.*

Once he is on the table, we remove the leash from Moxie's collar and hold a tidbit over the chair seat. It is just the right height that he can, by standing on his hind legs and stretching, comfortably reach it.

Moxie takes the tidbit, backs down and eats it. I hold another over the chair seat and, as Moxie stretches up to get it, click a cricket. After this reinforcement is consumed, I hold the next one so high that he can't reach it, making it necessary for him to jump. As he does, he hears the cricket and instantly tastes the reinforcement which he eats without jumping down.

I upset his balance and he jumps down. In Moxie's case, I click and he hops up at once. He is partly conditioned. Having eaten his tidbit, down he goes and at the sound of the click, up he goes again. We repeat this twenty times.

At the next session, it required only a sniff of the reinforcement to evoke memories of the last session, and Moxie got twenty more conditionings. To him the click meant to jump up, whether on the table or onto the chair.

We have another child's antique chair which you can see in the illustration. I thought it would be interesting to determine what his reaction to it would be if I substituted it for the high chair. I clicked, and, to my surprise, Moxie jumped onto it, but not by the proper avenue. He turned around, sat with his paws on the back, and waited expectantly for his tidbit.

Lesson 6. To Pray

This is a party trick and of little value because no one can tell whether the cat is really praying. I used Moxie for this demonstration because he had learned to jump onto the chair.

If you want to condition your cat to pray in public instead of within the confines of her private room, here is how you do it:

First condition her to jump onto a chair with a low enough back so that her paws can hook onto it and her chin rest upon it too, with at least a show of comfort. Hold the reinforcement over the chair's back and as she reaches for it lower your hand so

We put a tidbit on the chair seat and say CHAIR *as he reaches for it.*

By holding the reinforcement we get him to jump and we say CHAIR *as he does.*

After a few repetitions he responds.

Now we can stand away from the table and, at hearing CHAIR,
our pupil jumps up and seems to ask, "Where's my tidbit?"

When we tried a child's chair to test his response to CHAIR *Moxie jumped onto it but from the wrong direction.*

He jumps down at our signal DOWN.

It takes many repetitions to have him get on the chair in a gentlemanly way.

her throat is touching the chair back. The instant she reaches this position pop the tidbit into her mouth and at the same time say *Pray*.

Repeat this process half a dozen times or more if necessary until you say *Pray* and she holds the pose. Delay offering her the reinforcement, which she can see held below and out of her reach, longer and longer. When she responds perfectly, repeat it twenty times. Go through the same procedure twenty more times at the next session.

Lesson 7. To Sit Up

Waldo was conditioned to sit up but not as easily as one might think. If you try this with your cat, you too may find that training her to sit and not extend paws upward, trying to reach for the tidbit, is not so simple.

Fasten your cat so she can have some liberty on the table top without jumping off. Hold the tidbit over her head. She will sit up and reach for it. She will probably jump toward your hands. If she is not a gentle cat she may hook her claws into your hand, so watch out.

Close your fist about the tidbit. Hold the closed fist over her head and when she sits up without extending her paws say *Sit* and open your hand and give her the tidbit. That worked well with Waldo.

Just seeing your hand over her head and hearing *Sit* as she sits up soon conditions her. Raise your hand higher and higher above her. She will realize that she can't reach it and will sit steadily. Soon you can say *Sit* without holding your hand above her, as I soon did with Waldo, and your cat too will respond by sitting. But to condition her, you will patiently have to repeat the response twenty times.

Our pupil prefers to stand when he sees the tidbit.

But soon he sits, hears the signal and takes the reinforcement.

He has heard the signal as he started to sit. Now he sits and waits for the tidbit to come to him.

Even with the tidbit held high above him he sits in response to the signal.

He is becoming conditioned, just looks at the trainer and hopes to have his want—hunger—fulfilled.

Now he will respond every time to the sound of the signal.

Lesson 8. To Shake Hands

The illustration shows a part of my cat colony. Please note that several cats are reaching out of their cages to get something they want. What? Food? You would naturally think so. But in every cage there is a pan of excellent, savory food, and a dish of water. Those cats want to be scratched. They don't itch; they just love to have me rub their ears and scratch their backs. Here's how this behavior started.

As I was carrying a food dish to a cat when she was hungry, she put her paw out to reach the dish. Instead of giving her the food, I opened the door, reached in and scratched her ears. Then I gave her the food but instead of eating it, she put out her paw again. So I scratched her and said *Shake*. I tried it with other cats and before long I could say *Shake* and out would pop many paws. I was supplying a need.

A boy who was working for me set a trap in the woods to catch a woodchuck for the Nature Center, but he caught, instead, a yellow cat. He was badly clawed when removing her from the boxtrap into a burlap sack. Knowing I needed a cat, he brought her to me more as a joke than anything else. She presented a real challenge. She was a furious animal when frightened, even worse than the cat I caught in my Havahart trap. And she remained frightened for almost a week, drinking her water but refusing all food.

We sarcastically called the cat Sweetheart. But today the name fits her and the change which came over her began by shaking hands. After two weeks she had learned that we would not harm her even when the pan was changed every other day. She ate well and was a good food tester but resented my hands, backing into a corner, bristling, and hissing when the door was opened.

I decided to try to tame her. I gave her no food for thirty-six hours and when I offered it, held it outside the cage. She reached for it, and I gave her a morsel quickly and said *Shake*. Each time she reached, she got a morsel and heard *Shake*. She responded after a few more trials as if she couldn't help it. Actually she

*One section of the author's cat colony. Most of the cats shake
hands.*

couldn't. So I opened the door and put the food inside. She was backed in the corner but not bristling. I said *Shake,* and her paw came forward, and she ate her tidbit. This was repeated until she had responded twenty or more times. She was by then no longer afraid of my hand.

From there on it was easy. Soon she would stand in the door and let me scratch her ears, but as I drew my hand away, out would come a paw, showing she wanted more rubbing. Yet she never extended her nails. Two years later this same behavior occurs. She is a *real* sweetheart, loves to be handled, and is one of the finest cats I own.

So now let's see how to accomplish it with *your* cat!

The black cat used in our illustrations is, again, Waldo. He had been a pet and required almost no ear rubbing to establish a sympathetic relationship. He learned to jump onto the table at the sound of the clicker almost as if he had been previously conditioned, which he had not.

Pupil learning to shake hands, can't reach the food with his mouth so he extends a paw, hears SHAKE.

As you can see he was fastened so that his shoulders were even
with the front of the table. He was hungry, and when he smelled
the tidbit in my hand, reached for it eagerly. Immediately he did
so I said *Shake* and fed him the tidbit for reinforcement.

After a dozen repetitions he responded to the word *Shake*.
From then on he became conditioned until he would sit and
shake even when he was back from the edge of the table. In a
second session he was exercised twenty times, and now he shakes
hands any time he hears the word *Shake*.

He tries again, hears SHAKE *and gets a taste of tidbit.*

He still pulls on his leash but is learning as he hears the signal.

Soon he will be shaking quickly whenever he hears the word—the signal.

Lesson 9. To Pull a String

A friend of mine owns a cat that pulls a string to ring a bell. The bell notifies someone in the family that the cat wants to come in. This useful idea prompted me to condition two of my cats to pull a string.

There's a difference between a cat playing with a string and a cat pulling on a string in order to obtain something it wants. Yet the act of pulling the string from desire to play or from curiosity can be converted quickly and easily into a useful act both to the cat and the owner. Why shouldn't a cat, after she has been outdoors for a while, let her owner know that it's time to come back in, and do it without scratching the paint off the door or making holes in the screen?

I found two methods of conditioning two of my cats to pull the string. The first required more time than the second, but both methods are practical, so I'll describe them, and you can take your choice.

The first cat, Floosie, learned her lesson the longer way. I tied her so she could not jump off the table. She lay down peacefully but soon her curiosity was piqued by the end of a green string dangling in front of her nose. The string actually ran from a screw eye I had attached to the ceiling. I held the other end of the string so I could pull it up from the cat when necessary.

Floosie batted at the string, as any hungry or curious cat would. Nothing happened. She batted again, catching the end in her paw. Something happened: a juicy piece of warm corned beef dropped in front of her. It was the size of a postage stamp and almost as thin. She seemed surprised, and there was an increase in her alertness.

Several minutes passed before she took another swing at the string, but as she pulled it ever so slightly a second tidbit dropped before her. Floosie took at least ten minutes to associate the string with the food, but when she mastered it, she approached it with gusto.

We let her work at it until she was no longer hungry. From

Floosie I learned that much can be accomplished with conditioning by offering her tidbits of different sizes. Remember that a cat doesn't gulp food, she takes it into her mouth and really masticates it. The larger the tidbit supplied to the cat, the longer she requires to eat it. In Floosie's case I started off with tiny reinforcements and gave larger ones when she was working well at string pulling. Each time she took a large piece, 1 inch square by a quarter-inch thick, she took many seconds to chew and swallow it. This gave us time for our flash to recycle and for us to prepare for the next photograph, as well as for Floosie to give her attention to the food rather than the string.

That was the extent of my training Floosie. I taught her that when she pulled the string, she was given some food. But consider the possibilities! Now that she had learned this much, suppose the string was hung outside the back door and when she pulled it the door was opened by you!

Mrs. Whitney suggested that this was a poor trick to teach a cat. "Suppose a pet cat learned it, imagine the havoc in the house!" She was right. Every end of string or thread hanging from a knitting basket or from a ball, into which the cat could sink her claws would be pulled. "Anyway," my wife suggested, "You can't just hang a string outside; it would get wet in a storm and shrink. Moreover it would soon become frayed and have to be replaced."

This thoughtful remonstrance led to conditioning Waldo to pull a string with a little metal square attached to its end. In addition I tied a little tinkle bell on the string up near the ceiling. Any disturbance of the string caused the bell to ring.

In a loop of the string, next to the square, I put a tidbit of roast beef. It took Waldo several minutes to realize it was there. But when he did take it in a paw and bite it, the bell tinkled. Eight times I had my photographer friend lift Waldo away while I placed another tidbit in the loop. The ninth time Waldo went to the string, hooked a claw into the square and chewed on the empty loop which had a taste of roast beef, probably from the fat flavor. At once I popped a tidbit before him. He ate it

Our pupil learns to pull a string by first getting acquainted with it.

and returned to the job of playing with the square. Each time the bell rang. After a dozen such repetitions, I waited until Waldo was well away from the string and then jogged it to make the bell ring. Immediately his attention was called to the string where the tidbit was in the loop.

I let a few minutes elapse while Waldo was kept on the floor. Now I said *Up*. He was instantly back on the table and went directly to the string, pulled it, and received his reinforcement from my hand.

Thus both of my wife's objections were overcome. The string was not merely a string but a metal square (it could as well have been a baby's teething ring), and the cat was not pulling on a string, so we were not conditioning our pupil to pull any available string. Moreover, if this were outside of a door which the cat wanted to have opened, he could grasp a solid object on its end.

He hooks his claws on it and hears a bell ring, eats the tidbit stuck in the metal square.

With no tidbit in the metal, he pulls on the string, hears the bell ring and sees a tidbit drop in front of him.

*After a few responses, a string with a metal square on it means
something good. He even tugs it with his mouth.*

Lesson 10. To Stand

Cats do not sniff around to locate food; they use their eyes for this purpose. You can take advantage of this fact in teaching your cat to stand up. But if she is like mine you will have to be patient and put up with a lot of reaching with her paws and jumping up to touch the tidbit you hold above her head.

I found it was a simple response to teach but easiest when done in two sessions. Moxie was the cat again. It required twelve minutes before he responded to my signal of two clicks on the cricket. I held a tidbit up as high as I thought he could reach but he must have decided this wasn't worth trying for and made no attempt to rise to the bait. Then I lowered my hand so that he could try and as he did so, clicked twice. He dropped down, chewed his tidbit and after swallowing, looked up again at my hand. When he thought he could reach it he stood up again. Each time my hand was held higher and each time he stood up he heard the click. As I said, by twelve minutes he would stand at the sound of the click and I would bring my hand downward and reinforce his action. But notice that when he stood up he also reached as high as he could with his paws.

All I wanted was for Moxie to stand on his hind legs when I clicked twice, so I concluded the lesson at this point and began there the next session. After a few responses with my hand within reaching distance (he responded readily), Moxie started learning to stand with his arms at his side. However, no matter how many times I handed him his tidbit, after each response to the clicker, he always brought his paws up and held them against my hand until he had taken his tidbit.

After many responses I next put Moxie on the floor to see if the conditioning would be effective there. No, Moxie began exploring every part of the room and beneath the table. Having satisfied himself there was nothing more to interest him, he came before the camera and looked up at me. I clicked twice, and up he stood.

As a first step in learning to stand on his hind legs, hungry Moxie sees the tidbit and as he rises hears the signal.

He reaches higher, again hears the signal, again his action is reinforced.

Moxie wants to be certain of his tidbit.

He rises higher on his legs each time he hears the signal.

Now he has associated signal and reinforcement.

He's right up there now and will respond every time to the signal.

There is another way of conditioning for this response, which I learned accidentally. Having Floosie tied on the table, I had forgotten to remove the string from the screw eye in the ceiling and it hung down about a foot over where the cat's head would be if she stood up. Floosie happened to look up at the large bow I had made. Curiosity caused her to stand up toward it. I happened to have some reinforcement handy and the clicker, so I clicked and offered her the tidbit, bringing my hand down from the bow knot. We stood back and sure enough up she stood again. Each time she heard the click and received the tidbit she would stand up.

Whether this method of conditioning works with your cat will depend upon whether you can arrange something above her and about which she would be curious. Perhaps an imitation mouse, which you could jiggle to get her attention, would accomplish it.

Lesson 11. To Climb a Ladder

Climbing and jumping up are quite different actions. In the case of all of the cats, one signal on the clicker or *Up* was used to condition them to jump up on the table. Some responded to the signal only when I was facing the table. Bickle and Moxie would jump up no matter where I was in the room or in what position. As there is no point in training a cat to jump up on a height without some purpose, it is probably better to condition him as I did.

I thought it would be interesting to place a ladder on the floor against the table and, instead of jumping, train the cat to climb the ladder at a signal. This was accomplished with little Bickle (for bi-color). Bickle had been brought to the Whitney Clinic by an agent of P.A.W.s to see if a home could be found for him; if not—. A home was found. Strangely, Bickle had been fed a can of cat food and some of the uneaten food remained in his cage when I took him. His reinforcement consisted of tiny tidbits of fried beef, and he responded to it as most cats do only when they are thirty-six-hours hungry.

Instead of having to bend over I placed a household ladder on

He finds out there is a tidbit when he responds to the signal and comes to the first step.

Now he has discovered the second step.

the table. Bickle was put on top to determine whether he was used to such a perch and, as you can see, he jumped down the moment I withdrew my hands. Now we had a job to do—condition Bickle to climb without fear and sit on the top.

This was accomplished with tidbits and a cricket. I placed a tidbit on the first step, and as Bickle took it, I clicked. He walked away, but when he was looking toward my hand, I dropped another on the step and clicked as he was walked toward it and also when he took it. At least ten repetitions were necessary before he would hurry back to the step at the sound of the click. Ten times more this was repeated and by that time he hurried right to the step at the sound. Each time he received his reinforcement, which was supplying what he wanted.

Now for the next step. When he came at the clicker's sound, he found no tidbit on the lower step. I held a tidbit over the edge of the second step. He reached up for it, and I clicked as he did so. It was easy now. If no food was on the first step when the clicker sounded it was on the second. Without any further conditioning I showed him there was reinforcement on the top step.

But Bickle wouldn't climb up for it; he simply stood on his hind legs and reached with his paw. Naturally I put the tidbit just out of his reach, and he learned that only by climbing could he reach it. He put a hind foot on the bottom step and found he could reach the tidbit; he also heard the click. But he was timid about the height and kept looking around, undecided as to whether to try or jump down.

When he responded to the clicker and found the tidbit whenever he climbed up, the next step naturally was for me to hold the tidbit up so high he couldn't reach it. I clicked and Bickle came all the way up, sat, and reached with a paw for the tidbit. The conditioning previous to the clicking and having learned to climb up, plus his having learned that the ladder was safe, combined to reassure the cat, and now when I clicked he climbed up and sat on the top.

The next lesson was twenty-five-times repetition. Before it was completed, the ladder was placed on the floor beside the table. Bickle was placed on the floor. He had never been conditioned to jump on the table. Now he heard the click and at once gave up exploring the room, climbed up the ladder, and onto the table.

You can teach your cat just as easily. I suggest that you teach it to sit, and after it has been taught to climb a ladder, to sit when it reaches the top and is commanded to do so. Any ladder will do. A ladder with six steps can be used. Just so your cat knows that clicking means *Climb,* it will climb your six-step ladder and sit on the top—and learn to do it with alacrity. Try it and have some fun.

So far we have been discussing our cats' education in the room we have set apart for that job. Suppose you have conditioned your cat to respond to many signals, but always in this one area; now what will she do in a different environment? You'd like to exhibit her prowess to friends. Must you take them to the training room?

It is well, after each response has been learned in the training room, to have your cat respond to your signal in a different environment. Once a cat has been properly conditioned, she will respond almost anywhere. But at first she will respond less quickly in a new environment. She may want to look around and take in her surroundings.

What to her was a specific chair or table is the one she expects to jump on at your signal. Now you must show her that *chair* means any chair you want to use. For other responses, exercise your cat on the living room floor until she will respond in a variety of environments. When she does that, show her off, and your friends will be astounded. If they own cats, whether or not your name is Jones, they will try to keep up with you.

Up he climbs and finds his tidbit on the top step.

He reaches the top, has been reinforced but finds the height is scary.

Now he climbs up in response to the signal and looks for his expected tidbit.

No longer uncertain, he has responded and has learned the lesson. Now for twenty or more repetitions.

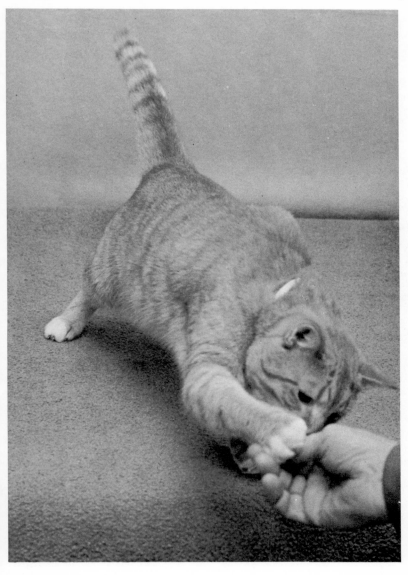

Moxie reaches for a tidbit.

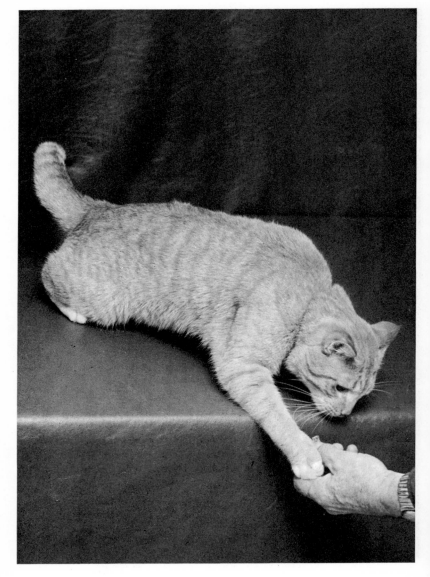

He must LIE DOWN *before he receives it.*

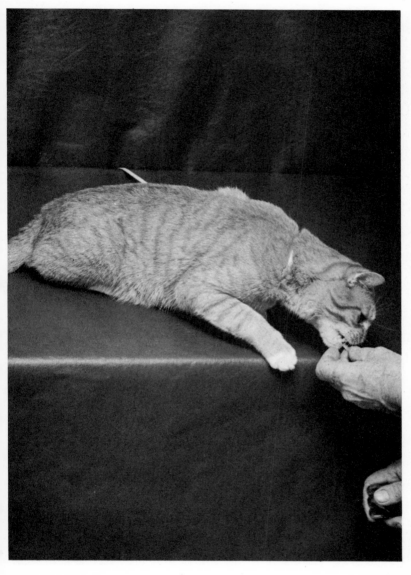

He hears the signal as he lies down and is reinforced.

After a few responses he drops at the signal and accepts his tidbit.

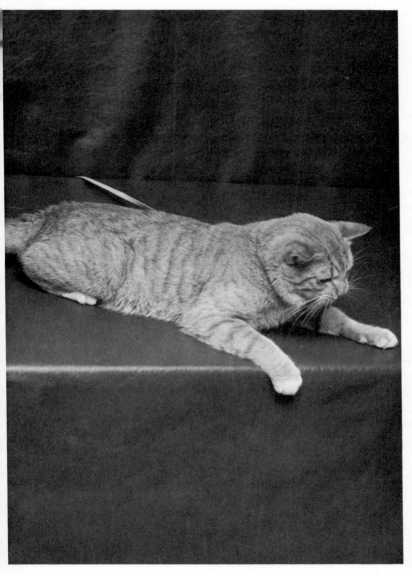

After a few more responses he lies down at the signal whether he sees or smells food.

Chapter Nine

Negative Conditioning

It is probably in keeping with the general idea that a cat cannot be trained, that when one speaks about the possibility of training one, thoughts turn to negative conditioning. "When my cat jumps on the table I sock it with a fly swatter," or "Say, by the way, how does one stop a cat from urinating against the wall?"

In this chapter we shall discuss negative conditioning which is, in a sense, mild brainwashing. As I said in an earlier chapter usually it is mistakenly used to indicate precisely the opposite of its real meaning. We read that the Communists have brainwashed a person. They really know how to do it. Brainwashing is one method of eradicating conditioning.

As far as I can determine the basis for true brainwashing was discovered in Pavlov's laboratory in Russia. His dogs were kept in the basement. All of them were extremely valuable, highly conditioned animals, trained with meticulous care. A flood occurred, and the water rose rapidly when a river overflowed its banks. All hands in the laboratory worked to save the valuable instruments and forgot the dogs. All of these animals had been caged in enclosures that reached to the ceiling. As the water rose the dogs had to swim and cling to the sides of the enclosures to keep from drowning. After hours of this panic there was only a little air space left up near the ceiling. A worker remembered the dogs. He swam under water, unlatched the doors, and one at a time pulled the dogs to safety.

All of these dogs proved to be so completely brainwashed that they knew nothing, failed to respond to signals, were practically vegetables and had to be completely re-educated. Such an experience is patently nothing like conditioning.

There are however, less drastic methods of extinguishing learned responses. The fly swatter is one simple way of keeping the cat off the table. If, every time she hops up, she is slapped, however gently, her conditioning to jump up becomes extinguished slowly, very slowly.

Here we must explain that the rapidity of the brainwashing depends on the severity of the deconditioner. Suppose that the cat, instead of jumping onto the table, landed instead on the electric stove on which a grate was turned on and she burned a foot. With a howl she would jump off. This one negative conditioning would be more effective in keeping her off the stove than many mild taps with the fly swatter.

Negative conditioning can come about by lack of use, but this is a slow method and a few positive responses to the old habit will activate the old habit again. Suppose you have trained your cat to stay off the table, and sometime when you are away she smells a goody and jumps up. She received no slap. Soon she is back at it again, perhaps only when you are away. And if she "gets away with it" when you are home, she will be a regular jumper.

With this explanation what do we do to correct—to decondition—a cat whose habits we do not like?

The Word NO!

How often have you seen a cat to whom the owner used the word No with effect? Not often, and yet all cats can be conditioned to appreciate that this word means *stop what you are doing*. It is only a matter of the cat realizing the undesirable consequences of her doing something you feel she should not do. When she touches a glowing ember, the act carries its own consequences. Biting an electric wire and feeling a violent shock is such severe negative conditioning that one trial cures the cat of biting any wire.

Try to think about that when you decondition. It does no good to threaten, like the ignorant mother who says to the misbehaving child, "Wait until your father comes home." In the case of the cat the negative conditioner, the pain, if you will, should be part of the action. Let only a few seconds pass and the cat does not connect the action with the pain. It should be like an electric shock which the cat feels as a consequence of biting the wire, or the pain in her paw which touched the ember. And remember what we said about the severity of the deconditioner and the speed of learning what was wrong to do.

What are some of the things you can do that the cat will learn to associate with misbehavior? A slap with your open hand is one, a hard slap with a rolled newspaper another. The strong fly swatter made of plastic, not wire, is one of the best negative conditioners ever invented. I've seen a cat's eye which has been punctured with a piece of loose wire on a screen wire type swatter, so I believe it is a dangerous tool.

A plastic fly swatter is indeed a tool which you can use in such a way that the impression the misbehaving cat gets is that it is part of the wrong act. There is a flexibility and spring to it; it is gentle yet positive. It frightens more than it hurts. But if you let a few seconds pass, let alone a minute or more, all you do is make your cat afraid of you.

You see your cat about to jump on the table, you grab for the swatter, and just as she comes up, pow! She gets a slap in the face and hears the word *No!* Only a few repetitions are necessary before she understands *No* in that connection.

Or she torments you because she trained you to feed her when she yowled in front of your refrigerator and you want no more of it. What do you do? Why, every time she yowls, you smack her and say *No!* After a few repetitions of this, yowling or even standing before the refrigerator will be the same as calling you to come and smack her. You'll be amazed how quickly her habit will be extinguished.

Other negative conditioners have been proposed, such as shaking a little pepper on the cat. Another is the use of a spray with obnoxious content.

Keeping a cat away from a fish tank should be no problem, because every tropical fish tank should be covered with a glass top. Goldfish bowls can be covered with a wire screen to encourage evaporation, which cools the water, and that is what the inhabitants need, since they are actually cold-water fishes.

A cover of any kind over the tank or bowl protects the fishes, and the cat, finding she cannot reach them, and receiving a smack from your fly swatter whenever you find her up near the tank, where she doesn't belong, will soon lose interest.

To Stay Off Furniture

The matter of keeping cats off furniture is a problem to some cat-owners but not to others. Some discourage and others encourage it. The word *furniture* takes on different meanings in this connection. A beautiful longhair cat draped along the top of a divan is a sight to excite admiration. But that cat walking among the plates, cups, and saucers of a newly set dining table is a cat out of place. Some plants are lovely in a flower garden but weeds in a cornfield.

The same cat nibbling on a plate of cold chicken on the kitchen table becomes a cat weed too. So furniture may mean chairs but not tables. And then there are those who want no cat hairs on chairs and deny their cats any and all furniture.

Suppose you are one who insists the cat stay on the floor. But you find, when you go out and return, a lot of cat hairs on the seat of one upholstered chair, how can you condition her to stay off it? Buy some carpet tacks about 5/8 to 3/4 of an inch long.

Procure a piece of strong heavy cardboard the size of the chair seat and press the tacks through it so there is one every inch all over it. Put it on the chair seat with the tack points up and cover it with a cloth. Then don't forget you put it there. If you leave the chair thus protected it will quickly discourage the cat. If she takes up her abode in another chair, move your tack-imbedded cardboard to that one.

Should she leave hair on your clothes or furniture, a rubber sponge will brush them off faster than a whisk broom, in case you didn't know.

Scratching Furniture

Hundreds of thousands of dollars worth of damage is done annually by cats that scratch furniture until the fabric is shredded or the wood clawed so badly that only expert refinishing can restore it. What to do to prevent it?

There are two methods commonly employed. First, a scratching post can be provided, and when the cat tries her claws on anything else, punish her by a hard swat with a strong fly swatter, or, if she knows the word *No*, say that as she is getting ready to scratch. And never let an exception occur.

The other method is to have all of her front nails removed, or perhaps only the middle two on each front foot. In my practice I removed only the middle two, and clients reported excellent results. However, I have heard of cats on which this operation was performed that were such incorrigible scratchers that they had to be returned to have the remaining nails removed.

To Stop Predating

There is a difference between predating and pre-dating. Cats do not indulge in the latter, but as predators they are often notorious. If you permit it—the killing of wild animals and birds—you run an excellent chance of losing your cat.

How? Well, once a cat learns he or she can live comfortably

on nature's foods with no human help, that cat frequently goes away for increasingly longer periods and finally becomes wild. In this case the proper word is *feral*. Everybody knows that feral cats live by catching birds, and as usual, "everybody" is wrong. In the stomachs of hundreds of feral cats trapped by game wardens, there were occasional feathers but the great bulk of the contents was of rodents. At some seasons there were more game birds, as if the cat could have caught sitting birds. So hunters swear revenge. Part of the job of game wardens in some states is the trapping of wild cats. Thousands are trapped or shot every year, but the numbers of feral cats are constantly augmented by tame cats who leave home.

So it is obvious that no cat should be encouraged to catch any live creature other than rodents. He should not include squirrels, for several reasons. The first is that squirrel killing is the apprenticeship to becoming so expert at natural living that your cat doesn't need you any longer and goes wild. The other reason is that your neighbor may like squirrels and may feed and make pets of them. When he sees your cat kill one of his pets, he may put a rifle bullet through the cat or catch him in a silent Havahart trap.

He may, as I do, own some pigeons as a hobby. He may find your cat in his loft and a few fifty-dollar pigeons dead. In that case you will wonder for a long while whatever became of your cat. I know every one of my neighbors' cats. I also own a Havahart trap. You'd be surprised to know how many, not my neighbors', I have caught in that trap, every one of which must have lived a long way from our home which is in sparsely settled suburbs. Cats will be tempted to eat birds, but catching birds is not easy. You may have a neighbor who dotes on feeding and studying wild birds. If your cat slinks about the feeder trying to catch birds on the ground that are eating spilled food, you will probably receive a phone call.

No cat should be a nuisance. The old, so frequently heard term, "putting the cat out at night" should never mean for all night as it formerly did and still does for some. The place for the cat is under your control at all times and when she no longer is, you should not complain when you lose her.

How does one stop a cat from predating? By keeping her under control. When you put her out, watch her until she has dug a hole, relieved herself and covered it, and then call her in. Or use a string with a bell attached and condition her to pull it and let you know she is ready to come in. If she doesn't return within a reasonable time, call her in.

What if she is an uncontrollable predator? A farmer who had no emotional attachment to his barn cats would say, "Destroy her and get another." But we do have feeling for our cat, so what do we do? We keep such a cat on a leash and do not permit her to roam and kill. We condition her to respond to our call, and we know that the desire to kill will slowly become extinguished by lack of use.

The key word to the problem of the predating cat is *control*.

Chapter Ten

Housebreaking

In the case of a cat, the term *housebreaking* means more than simply conditioning her to eliminate in a certain place or to go outside for the purpose; Indeed, this is the simplest part of housebreaking. Cats can be very destructive animals when permitted to follow their natural bents, but they can be and are, in millions of homes, properly conditioned to become lovely and useful creatures. Yes, and excellent companions.

Lovely in the sense of beautiful, soft, graceful, adaptable, sweet. Useful as mousers and ratters, mole catchers, ears for deaf persons to notify them of persons at the door or when the telephone rings.

Even if cats were completely useless, as, alas, too many are, in the sense that they afford companionship, they serve a purpose. Few are the human beings, especially the lonely, whose lives are not enriched by having a live companion about. Even a poor goldfish kept unnaturally in a small, globelike prison and gradually fed to death or warmed to death, can be a companion.

Something alive to have about! To some, this may seem absurd.

But not to the lonesome person. And what more innocuous object
than a cat can such a person have?

You may have known of spoiled, unhousebroken cats kept
in certain homes, and so dispute this opinion of mine. Unhousebroken cats are not innocuous. Neither is your neighbor's dog,
who comes into your garden and digs up your prize lilies, but this
should not condemn the well-behaved dog. And the fact that a few
cats are untrained should not condemn all cats. This book's purpose is to insure that the keeping of cats be as pleasurable as
possible.

How can one manage the problem of elimination? Few animals
are more easily conditioned than the cat.

Remember that a cat instinctively digs a hole, defecates, and
then covers the feces. Keep a cat in a home with nothing to dig
in, and let her become frightened when she was outside behaving
naturally, and this fright will have conditioned her against going
outside. With no place to dig and cover naturally, she chooses
carpet or matting or even scratches at the bare floor. Of course
she claws the carpets into shreds! What else can she do?

If she has continued in this practice as the result of negligence
on the owner's part, she may prove refractive to housebreak. So
we have two problems: one, how to condition a new cat to our
home; two, how to correct the habits of the unhousebroken cat.

Remember the fact that when an animal is permitted to do
something which is the exercise of one of its natural instincts,
that act gives it pleasure. It fills a need. That's why one of the
things you need to do to condition a cat properly in this respect
is to feed it so that defecation is not painful; (in other words a
non-constipating diet), and to provide a suitable receptacle with
proper material to dig in and cover.

If a cat becomes seriously constipated so that defecation causes
pain, then whenever she does go to her pan and feels pain,
the pan can become associated with the pain. If she then goes
somewhere else and eliminates without pain, she has learned to
avoid the pan. So proper feeding is important in housebreaking.

What sort of pan should one provide? We conducted tests in

our cat colony to determine the answer. We tried cardboard boxes provided for the purpose, metal pans of both galvanized and stainless steel, and metal pans of various dimensions.

Where a great many cats are maintained in a colony, efficiency must bulk large in one's consideration. In the end we found that stainless steel pans eleven inches wide, eighteen inches long, and four inches deep were ideal. Shallower pans were less valuable about in proportion to their depth. We purchased a large number of pans two inches deep, and the cats scratched much of their sand over the edge. Inch-deep pans were worse. Very little sand —usually none—comes over the edge of a four-inch pan when there is an inch or one and a half inches in the bottom.

Why stainless steel? For two reasons: First, cat urine corrodes galvanized iron in a few months; it does not affect stainless steel. If we coated the galvanized iron with liquid plastic, it lasted longer.

Second, stainless steel pans are expensive, but all the sand, damp or sticky, comes off the bottoms and sides easily, whereas it sticks to galvanized iron and sticks much more when there are rust or corroded areas.

Why not cardboard? Because cardboard pans had too shallow sides and cats often clawed them. In a home they may have real merit because they can be discarded with the contents and replaced without any need of washing.

The material used in the bottom of pans is usually referred to as *sand*. Sometimes it is sand. Cats like to use sand. A box of nice dry sand can be stored and used until the need to replenish the supply. But more and more cat owners are turning to a better substance. This is commercial Fuller's earth which is used by garages to dry oil or other fluids spilled on the floor. In pet shops it may be purchased under a variety of names. One excellent type has had a deodorant to which cats seem not to object, mixed with the earth.

Some cat owners dig dirt from the garden to use in cat pans. Since it contains considerable moisture, it does not have the high absorbent properties of dry sand or Fuller's earth, and when it contains much fine clay, when damp it tends to stick to the cat's feet and leave track marks where she walks.

So much for the pans. How do we get a cat to use one? As I said, this is almost automatic, because the cat will usually search it out, once she knows that it contains good digging material. But how to introduce a new kitten to it? Just after the kitten has eaten, put her in the pan. If she jumps out and goes somewhere else to relieve herself, make a cage around it, using some plywood pieces in a corner of the room. Or you can put the pan and kitten in a bathtub. She can't climb out, and she will find the pan. After having used the pan two or three times, the kitten will usually seek it out. This won't work with a kitten large enough to jump out of the tub.

How do we housebreak an older unhousebroken cat? Put an extra amount of "sand" in the pan and arrange a cage so that the pan occupies half of the floor. Keep the cat in it for a week. When she finds so much pleasure in using the sand, she will be housebroken from then on.

Another consideration in this problem is the odor of feces. If your cat relieves herself under your bed, you'll generally decide, "She ain't worth it." But, did you know that this odor can be controlled very nicely by the kind of food you feed? Yes, that makes all the difference. In this field I've had years of experience with my own cats and seeing and smelling the effects of foods.

Fresh fish, fresh meat, and many canned foods cause the obnoxious odor we associate with cat feces. Now several excellent dry foods can be obtained which cats do not usually relish as much as they do food you prepare for them, but these foods keep them in excellent health, form soft, normal stools, produce a minimum of odor, and have many virtues when it comes to housebreaking. In one of my cat rooms there are twenty-four cats. If we are studying a canned food in comparison with another, it is imperative that all the pans be changed every forty-eight hours, or the odor is too obnoxious. In contrast, two complete dry foods being compared will often produce so little odor that one cleaning in three days is sufficient. In the case of urine the greater the protein content of the food, the more the ammonia odor from the urine is noticeable.

Some of the semi-moist cat foods, like the dry type, produce stools much less obnoxious than canned or fresh foods. And this is a consideration in cat housekeeping not to be overlooked.

Cats which were frightened by dogs and are afraid to go outside are a problem when one lives where the outside is available to them. How can such a cat—and there are many such timid ones—be conditioned to go outside? Of course the cat can be fed indoors, put out at once, and not allowed to come in for long periods of time. But when there are dogs about, this is cruel. True, experienced cats may even enjoy being chased by dogs, but pampered house cats do not and become terrified of the outdoors. If you are certain that there are no dogs to frighten her, put the cat on a leash and tie her out to a stake until she has voided. A few cat-owners have an overhead wire with a trolley on it to which the cat's leash is attached. Then one always knows where to find the cat.

A trolley over a lawn is not as successful as it is over a sand box from which the sand is frequently removed and renewed.

An imperative reason for changing the sand is that intestinal parasites—especially hookworms—are so easily transmitted from one. The eggs hatch in the damp warm sand and the larvae work up to the surface of the soil from where they can bore through the skin of the cat's feet. Or the cat will lick her feet and ingest hookworm larvae or roundworm eggs.

Fleas also hatch from flea eggs in warm sand and the young fleas jump onto the cat. Fleas may have infected themselves with tapeworm eggs, so that when the cat swallows an infected flea, she soon has tapeworms. It pays to change the sand at least once a week in the sand box under the trolley.

When several of my friends knew that I was writing this book each one urged me to be sure and explain how to train a cat to use the bathroom john instead of a pan. It is not as silly as it sounds. Many a cat has learned by herself to jump into

the bathtub and urinate over the drain, an action which is tolerated
by many cat-owners—but not all.

The entire question of defecation and urination is really a matter
of a cat's filling a need, the need she feels to be relieved. Just
the act of relieving herself is fulfilling a need and this is built-
in reinforcement. If the cat associates something with the act
while she is having her need fulfilled, she will repeat that
act. When she was a tiny kitten she had a need to be relieved
but she was not relieved until her mother licked her. This was
the signal to relax the muscles that held her urine and feces from
passing out. If it were not for this co-operation between mother
cat and her kittens, the nest would soon become filthy; but it
never is. The licking is the signal that triggers the action. Kittens
do not defecate or urinate in their nest.

After the kittens are old enough to walk out of the nest and
too old for mother to tend them, what is the next signal which
triggers their action? Probably the feel of the substance under
them to their feet. With no mother to stimulate them to relieve
themselves, their little bladders and rectums fill so full that they
must get relief. If they feel earth or sand or shredded paper as they
do let go, that substance under their feet becomes a signal, and
they will search for more next time they need relief. A cat brought
into a home new to it may "go" on a rug under the bed. When
it does, the reason is usually that it had previously been conditioned to use carpet usually by lack of discipline by its former
owner. Even little kittens instinctively scratch to cover what they
have done. But old cats can lose this instinct and care nothing
for a pan of sand or sandlike material. For some reason they have
become brainwashed-deconditioned. They can however become
reconditioned to use a pan. Because they no longer need to
scratch and cover, they can now be trained to use the john.

You can't sit your cat on the seat and tell her to "go." But
you can first train her to use a wire screen which covers her
pan. She must be a pan user. So you obtain a piece of wire
cloth with one inch squares of so-called turkey wire with one by
two inch openings. Cut it to fit over the pan with the edges bent

down so it can't fall off. Your cat, finding she cannot reach the sand, will make an attempt, but the pan is in the accustomed place, so she will sit on the wire and relieve herself.

After she has done this for a few weeks, move the pan next to the john. A week later put another piece of wire over the seat of the john and take away the pan. She has become conditioned to using the wire in a certain place. So now she finds it on the john. You may find her crying about the place where the pan was. She needs relief, so gently place her on the wire. When she relieves herself there many times it has become a matter of defecating in this place and the wire can then be removed.

Chapter Eleven

The Problem of Neutering

The word *neuter* as applied to most cats is a misnomer; it is, in a sense, a word used by nasty-nice persons who refuse to say *castration*. It's like being reticent about calling a female dog a bitch, which it is. Almost all cats, toms and cattas alike, are castrated either when they have reached maturity or close to that time. Actually, most cat-owners don't know whether they own a tom or a catta until they smell the acrid odor of the mature tom's urine, or fail to smell it. Perhaps one of the reasons for the popularity of the calico or tortoise-and-white cat is that the public knows they are always females. A few tricolors have been males but so few that they make news.

Perhaps you don't realize that this question is pertinent to the problem of cat education, but it is, especially in the case of toms. So you should know the following facts.

The word *castration* can be applied to the removal of a tom cat's testicles or a catta's ovaries, but we usually refer to the operation in the catta as spaying because it is more than simply removal of the ovaries; it involves hysterectomy, removal of the uterus *and* the ovaries. The medical term is ovario-hysterectomy.

If the operation is performed when the animal is mature or almost mature, all of the body's glands will have had an opportunity to have produced a normal male or female. One cannot tell by looking at a tom that was castrated when he was just mature whether he had been castrated or not. Nor can one tell from the general female appearance of a catta whether she has been spayed. So the word *neuter* is inappropriate.

The word *is* appropriate if either operation is performed very early in the kitten stage. In such cases, the ovaries of the catta are gone so that they cannot function along with other glands and produce the female characteristics we have come to associate with a normal female cat. Such cats are somewhat larger than unaltered cattas.

The castrated tom never grows to have typical tomcat characteristics, like wide jowls. He has a kinder expression and less tendency to fight.

The behavior too, is greatly affected. The catta has no periods of calling for toms, no rolling about and assuming, to us, grotesque positions. The tom has no tendency to urinate against an object but continues to squat to urinate as he did when he was a kitten.

Now he is much less inclined to hunt but becomes a stay-at-home. The calling of neighbor's cattas holds no attraction to him. He is much less inclined to become a wild cat. This is one of the most important considerations. Toms in the surburbs or country drift into wildness gradually. First they heed the call of a neighboring catta. Soon they drift off to farther farms in search of love. Anyone who has driven on lonesome country roads, sometimes miles from any farm, will remember the prowling cats he has seen beside the road and wondered whether they were wild. Not necessarily. This propensity has given rise to the expression: "He lives so far back in the country that he has to keep his own tomcat." That's far back, considering the distances toms have been known to roam. Castration puts an end to the urge to roam.

We use the word *neutering* to apply to cats of both sexes which were operated on early in life. The surgery produces cats that become intersexes, looking neither like males or females.

The problem of negative conditioning is very much concerned with surgery, or whether we are dealing with normal cats or those without testicles or ovaries. I have discussed the subject because I have been asked so many times by persons whom one would expect to know the answer. "How can I stop my cat from wetting against the wall? She has only just started and her urine is getting stronger all the time." Or, "What can I feed my cat to make her urine smell less strong?"

I have had to tell them they must have toms, which always surprises them. In the event you don't know how to tell a tom kitten from a catta, the old maxim is useful: under the tom's tail it looks like a colon (:), while the catta looks like a semi-colon (;). That's a pretty good description in a kitten. The anus in both is the upper dot, while the opening for the penis of the tom in a kitten looks like a dot. The vulva of the catta, corresponding to this lower dot is a line. So now when you select your kitten you won't have to rely on color but can choose on the basis of anatomy—or punctuation! Should you be uncertain when the pet is mature, if it is a tom, you'll find a testicle on each side of the colon (o:o). If it is a tom, unless you need him as a breeder, then have him castrated, pronto, for your good and for his.

AFTERWORD

You now have enough information on how to educate your cat. Please use it. As a first step, go to the toy counter of a store and spend a few cents for a cricket. When you have brought it home, knowing what you do from having read this book, your curiosity will overpower you; you'll simply have to see how it works with cats.

Provided you've fasted your pet for thirty-six hours, it will work. And when you once see for yourself how well it works, you won't be content with conditioning for just one response. You'll be calling in friends to witness your achievement, you'll be so proud.

A small warning: You may fall down because you don't have your cat repeat the response enough times the first day and enough times at the next lesson two days later. If you don't complete the conditioning in this way, your pupil will not respond satisfactorily and invariably.

Your inclination will be to half teach one response and then go on to another. Don't. And don't forget to put your pupil through her repertoire of responses now and then, or they will become lost, extinguished, from lack of use. Those are my last words in this book. Now it's up to you.